Jake Sheff

The Rites of Tires

SurVision Books

First published in 2022 by
SurVision Books
Dublin, Ireland
Reggio di Calabria, Italy
www.survisionmagazine.com

Copyright © Jake Sheff, 2022
Design © SurVision Books, 2022

ISBN: 978-1-912963-37-9

This book is in copyright. No part of this publication may be reproduced, stored in a retrieval system, or transmitted in any form or by any means without the prior permission in writing from the publisher.

Acknowledgments

Grateful acknowledgment is made to the editors of the following, in which some of these poems, or versions of them, originally appeared, or are about to appear:

The Disappointed Housewife: "Exiter Riddles," "Recipe with Later's Salt for Lasters," and "In Warning Shot Attire"

Dumpster Fire Press: "A Pillar of Snow"

Fixator Press: "Why Tamper with the Spectral Spoil?"

Home Planet News: "Reading James Merrill at Bedtime"

Ink Pantry: "Two-Person Architect"

Melbourne Culture Corner: "An Apoplectic Paean to San Miguel de Allende"

Radius: "Desire is the Agent of Acquire"

Revolution John: "The thing that is poetic is the thing we're unaware of…"

Trampoline Poetry: "Creosote Covenant"

"On First Looking into a Sculpture of the Song…" was the winner of the 2017 Science Fiction Poetry Award

CONTENTS

Creosote Covenant	7
A Pillar of Snow	8
Exiter Riddles	10
Desire Is the Agent of Acquire	12
Recipe with Later's Salt for Lasters	13
Yukon Stranger	14
In Warning Shot Attire: A Game of Chicken	16
Two-Person Architect	18
Simulcast in Yon, Hermetic Orange	19
Reading James Merrill at Bedtime	20
The thing that is poetic is the thing we're unaware of...	22
Sending the Alphabet to the Back of the Line	24
Why Tamper with the Spectral Spoil?	25
Dear mid-November blues in early April...	26
An Apoplectic Paean to San Miguel de Allende	27
To Build an Icebox	28
Notes from a Textbook of Botanical Oncology	30
On First Looking into a Sculpture of the Song...	32

For my parents –
Your loving guidance keeps my honor's home.

Creosote Covenant

The fire truck is not the frotteurism dismantled by
parents to replicate on a rhizome-and-blues disc,
is not the satellite of Seattle's intended
nor a combination of gruesome celerity
and menarche without monocle or manacle,
but the implements are in place to rectify what-
ever, like some incorrect celery, comes our way.

None of this is writ on the to-do list of my cat
or any other legitimately enzymat-
ic grown up. It isn't carved, like some accusation,
in a heart with an arrow on some sturgeon or fir.
But whenever my wife's unheralded look of *You
turn on me, you turn me on* appears, it dwarfs all fires.

A Pillar of Snow

After John Ashbery, "Into the Dusk-Charged Air"

He used to walk a runway like a hotel with
an appetite, like India away from Taj Mahal.
The crowd was his sierra, tempting him
with exodus; a tango for an over-40 thrill.
He could've won an Oscar as the charming
side of March or Romeo, but the heart
cannot be dressed in Yankee Doodle genius.

Instead he kept a hotel in his eyes and Nissan
Altima. In India, a Chevy Malibu had washed
his feet with headlight madness. A Ford Sierra
lost its grip on reality by the light of his tan. Going
for Apollo's car, he blew a kiss to pull the sun
faster than an Alfa Romeo or winged minute. He
turned a Volkswagen Beetle's brain into a Yankee:

"Out, out –

The beauty spot – a stain
On man's eternal eye;
A fact – or two – are slain
To prove fertility"

He offered up tonight as a hotel for tomorrow.
India had taught him violence was a bad joke.
He wore the Sierra Madres to officiate all of
yesterday's tangoes with today, and vowed
to avenge tomorrow's death. (The o-shaped scar
on Romeo is from that ruined breath.) His
catwalk flowed into the Yangtze river out to sea.

Exiter Riddles

III.

I place my emphasis on penetrating
Matters: desiderata as the personal
Errata satiates my savagery, and I,
Its. Cynical, meticulous, the mapless
Man in white officiates my yaw,
These graceless arabesques into and through
Internalized, familiar song-and-dance,
The names and reproductions of delights,
Etcetera. The wizened wizardry I whiz by
Has taught me happiness exists in memory,
Prospect and art; the eternal returns of the sane.

VII.

I fenestrate placental and omphalic
Matters; the personality's deciduous,
Erotic eye that salvages and satirizes
Shit. Mellifluous and clinical as maples
That officiate my yawns, the man in black
Retraces introductions so familiar change,
Externalized by chance, becomes an airy bisque;
The shame of that electrical reduction is
Ecstatic. A weaselly and whistled wisdom
Has caught me Chaplinesque, resisting memory's
Respect for art, as the eternal's refurnishing flame.

Answers:

III. Scholars debate the answer to this riddle: a number have argued convincingly for "A bullet to the brain," while a not insignificant opposition has done likewise for "A poem."

VII. (See above)

Desire Is the Agent of Acquire

So chlorophyll desires light undead;
Mythology desires truth beheaded; rivers
Find desire urgently and prolix. Crows
Admit the loves they lost and storms
They swept, indifferent as the devil of
Possessing. Toads desire lily pads
And call it "paper rain," the feeling's
Place. The bulk of beauty seen but not
Desired demolished heights that proved
The all-effacing fathoms given heaven
Not mistaken, but incredulous to scrawny faith.

["Something great and god-like, not a man at all."
– On the question of subjects suitable
to verse, the author of *Cardioversion
and Other Lifesaving* **Measures.**]

So glory feels decidedly lightheaded.
My theology deserves the truth unsevered; ravens
Find it "surgically inspired." The crows' elixir
Abnegates the loaves they lost and crumbs
They wept; I'm different: bedeviled by
No ownership. The notepad's dotage calls
For ire; placid paupers reign with feeling
New desires. The biomass of dead ideas
Required hearts demoralized and moved
The stakes: the fathers, all ungoverned, scrawled
Their debts like heathen doubts on walls.

Recipe with Later's Salt for Lasters

*After "The Green Mountain White Ribbon Cook Book,"
published by the Woman's Christian Temperance Union
of Vermont, ca. 1895*

Flake the salmon into rather fine
endearments, sprinkling into it
a tiny pitch of trouble, arrange it in
a bowl garnished with latter-day
empiricism and pour over it
a dressing made of followers as
follows – 1 teaspoon of mustered
aggression, 4 teaspoons of pepper,
1 teaspoon of disputation, a pinch
of salty promises and cheeks to
grow an inch, add to this a table
of boiling wood, stir well, add two
tablespoons of better thoughts,
drop this into two unbeaten eggs,
and beat well enough to bitter.
Put over the fire, adding ¾ cup
of creamy constancy and one half
cup of vinegar – stirring evenly
to prevent cuddling or murder –
until thick like cream.
                    Thos. Bros., Geo. & Jos., of Springfield, Vt.

Yukon Stranger

You are like a remote control, dangerous (more than a mouse-pad). It doesn't even matter which you, or which part, or which two. You verb my vision, and afterwards it has feathers, a name, a rationale to get beat up, boarded up, as if hope itself was only a figure of speech. Adventure and discovery are always just beyond; extraneous to call this purpose, so you call it other ways. And language calls it you, its word synonymous with fence, homonymous with green, with no opposite, considered the most cathartic swear. Your life story conspicuously protects you like a bushy tail. Groom it with the others. You are the child of attention and faith, what you care about rebels, but someone is always pretending.

The epigenetic changes brought on by Pearl Harbor, the Holocaust, Nagasaki, are doomed to being ignored by the eye of existence if you don't save my life, disguised as the hollow moments within the building up of devotion. Don't ask yourself anything is good advice for an interior decorator they'll tell you. Life is the student and you're the school is a good truth to doubt, or good lie to believe, depending on the outcome, so goddamn unforeseeable.

What if you are a million clips on YouTube with the nouns and verbs separated, and the commenters "just don't get" your "handsome" and "retarded" modifiers? I am writing this prose poem about you because the world needs more you flatter it to unflatten it. Do you know what I mean by you, or what a cat means when it hears a mouse in the wall, or what the wall interprets to mean that? Imagine 99 bottles of Yoo-Hoo, but "you who" the question. Funny how sweet it tastes, how stupid and seminal.

In 2013 there was a "you" that twerked with a Higgs boson, then Tweeted about it which got 12 likes on Facebook. And you disintegrated when each of your cells took a selfie. You are always topical, and the you in universal. (Not to mention unicorn, and you are glad I didn't say eunuch.)

The End

is you, intermittently.

P.S. Beginning wants you on the International Space Station. But Worry and Worthy are being poached to extinction.

Yucatan Meddle
The title for reading this backwards

In Warning Shot Attire: A Game of Chicken

Based on the 1965–1966 rivalry between Bob Dylan and John Lennon

"My tea party is the peril, and this peril is very, very ordinary."
– Judy, played by Natalie Wood in "Rebel Without a Cause"

Jim:

No fraternizing fire lit Norwegian
Rum for the aroma; no gallant wine
Or thunderbolt to break your eye –
Or should I say, the bird that flew from
It – was sent to hum by tautologically:
That shit cray! Admiring a Gorky
Print, like protein for your grand mal
On stage, is fine and dandy – no boo-boo,
No crawl – but intercepting fairies
To submit them to a man's laughter
Is no keener crutch than bloody baths
Or rugs that bide a burning chair.

Buzz:

Ha! Your fellowship forgets Jamaican
Gum with dirt in it; your wooden armor
Brokered ears more like a trident –

Or should I say, the bird that flew from
A teleological point of view – than a drum
Bat-shit crazy. A *Porky's* film
Admixture, more protean than grandma's
Wheelchair or a dandelion's drawer full
Of buboes; no introspective furloughs
Manumit you from that suit of manslaughter
Catherine Keener called cute: that bloody bed
Of plugs that worked you like a shoo-in curfew.

Two-Person Architect

While doctoring the sun, my wife expounds
On gradients of moonliness called "love."
Attending raves in giant fields, she'd tell
Us, "Nothing is a drug," and drop it like
A mic. And neon lights berated costly
Nights, so full of naked, blaring animus;
If not, at least of intimations. Without
A wink of hesitation, a raccoon is
Digging through my trash outside; emaciated
Martian with an ear for the eraser, like
My wife, whose syllogisms overlapped with hope.

While proctoring tomorrows, Obama rounds
The radiance of spoonerisms up to one.
"Pretending saves a little space," he'd tell
Us (nothing like a bug), and pop it like
A collar; neonates conflated bossy
Rights – the pull of naked, blaring animus –
With tons of steely scintillations. Pick out
The pinkest nation: a cocoon is
Hugging the rough trash inside me, wasted,
Marshaling an iridescent pacer like
My wife, her syllogisms home with overwhelm.

Simulcast in Yon, Hermetic Orange

For BN

At the request of light, inscrutable
Uncertainty was cast aside, or shed
In deeper shelves than oceans have. Perforce
Is why some feel that light's arrival was
Delayed, although this wouldn't account for mounds
Of cactus needles making downy beds.
The light was something you teamed up with, a
Most natural fixation, lifting nothingness
To Gaelic hymns, aloft with starry birds;
And light-years dissipated in your hands.
The compact's metaphors arrayed themselves...

For PM

...To the effect that wood (disputable
If curtains flee the past) allied, and said
'Go bleep yourselves' like oceans have. Of course,
This lissome deal, that wood and imbeciles
Delight in, threw what would, in discount minds,
Be practice noodles in *our* wally heads.
The hardness sometimes put up beams, a
Most unnatural fixation, lifting nothingness
Beyond East Hampton: starboard; floating.
But participating light-years waived our plans
And commas gave our foray's halves what for.

Reading James Merrill at Bedtime

"For it is a truth, which the experience of ages has attested, that the people are always most in danger when the means of injuring their rights are in the possession of those of whom they entertain the least suspicion."
– Federalist No. 25, Alexander Hamilton (as Publius)

Among the fakers, this poem, "Mirror,"
seems no faker; more like myrrh
attempting not to shine
inside another day's meconium.
To see its epidermis
suggesting and enforcing terms,
the fullness thereof, crawling with spiders
and a great deal of intentionality,
is to admit I don't know jack.
Today has sickle
cell disease, and time is death's
pituitary gland and feathers.
But in this poem, I see the naughty sister
of perfection prove a kiss
is always slightly monstrous.
For something sweet as kisses never known,
this poem auditions
thunder's muted speech in history's Audi,
one or two standard deviations above Jerusalem
it rides and rustles.
The hour women are getting late breaks
into my house. It's one heckuva

hypothesis; this poem's "Come over
to my Overton
window," as nightmares break
into blossom. Unlike Hecuba,
this poem never seems less ridiculous
than when it speaks
from a place where nothing's temporary.
Not that slutty city, Life – so far,
its capital is Death – where anger
loves cartoons and grief, not conquering
or conquered, is more like love's
protagonist. Commercial waterways' removal
of Of from depth perception's seams
by day reflects how dreaming
darkens this poem and the door
like my father before me.
From such dissolution, much is solved:
my daughter, my revolver;
agitated distances coming to fruition
in the skies above Astoria: big fish
starring in the summer's
of summers just war. At first blush, this poem
portrays an ass, expounding
with the always healthy sounds
of independence, don't it?
Meanwhile, the donut of the mind –
rolling through this poem and uphill
to Philadelphia,
as if to feed whatever marmots
methought I heard in the wind's revolting rhetoric –
suspects it tastes of truth and method.

The thing that is poetic is the thing we're unaware of...

I. For the ritual

"It loses value soon as it's off the lot," is what they'll say of time, the moon. In what sense do absences not bombard you? At what pressure does a space combust into inchoate sense? The answers I've found have been particles and waves alive in the dead zone of a malformed retina. The questions were bleached until they developed resistance, kind of like I sought some definite land mass before I could be what I knew outside of experience. Without any eyes, without any seem at all, love is only.

II. What Sexual Intercourse would say about all that

Phooey, but without phooey there can be no Satan, no residence for virtue, no negation or erasure to cut our teeth on. Without is the perfect mode for an endeavor with a fruition end-goal. Death is designed to accommodate those willing to try. Casting nets: that is the image the blind quintessence has of us.

III. What Proof-in-all-Forms will write in its autobiography's preface

Being formless and omniscient is so inhuman, but it invented itself. Inverting chaos for poetry invests order and despair with air. My soul continues by countering life. In this way I recognized the face of skepticism was painted, seductive insofar as my self-doubt was pointed. What trickles then isn't seconds into minutes, but spirit into whatever's dying.

IV. ...*And cannot be*

Finally, I realize a just crime is never final, mercy casts an ambiguous shadow, and God was unprepared but fearless. The universe is never speechless: it metabolizes everything we feel, converts it into manna, the words of the unheard. And firstly, wisdom competes with minds despite having more than everything to gain.

Sending the Alphabet to the Back of the Line

Childhood is plural for *away*,
China's clay soldiers are shooting you with BBs.
Childhood is 1536 and King Henry's clemency,
The death-bird whistling a Baltic melody.
Childhood is memory's monstrosity
That thrives because it is deaf.
Oedipus Rex disdained the moon at its apogee,
Appealed daily to his legislature:
"Outlaw it being anything but new! My eye-
Sockets bleed in moonlight, soak my PJs,
Because I can see again *as a child*, okay?"
What John Smith sought was the rattlesnake's fontanelle;
1608: "My nostrils imply a new Bethlehem,
But at noon the settlers appear to me…mannequins."
Some dough boys were virgins; with gusto
They died in poppy fields and kissed Calliope's
Fingers, whose signature shot the air with curlicues.
Aquinas denied his cicatrix, as did Belthazar –
"To credit father's brand with our success!"
The end of childhood is the rainbow's unity
Of hostile, verisimilar illusions. (re: Howard Hughes.)
The end of childhood is a flashflood of gravy,
Or for some, an old, nude harpy crying, "You! You!"
The start of childhood is always tardy; not sex,
But a staggering of Who, What, When, Where and Why,
Like pawns. The start of childhood is the end of easy.

Why Tamper with the Spectral Spoil?

The string was hung above the ground –
31" long and 31" high. Below,
The compost pile, and under that
A *primum non nocere* agreement
Between the celibate intensity and
Verruciform, bantam network. (My skin
Like microfiche, this property
Anathema to lithium, Athena, random
Miracles.) The seven 1s and seven 0s
Ran above: retaliation's form of libel;
The postal industry's falsetto trait in mime.

The ground's gung-ho astringent, like a
13, cinches the quotidian by its one-and-thirty
Piles of short-and-curlies; and under,
Nociceptors: agriculture's double-ply
Phenomena, in tandem with celebrity
Intestines; the skein of net worth cruciform.
(The micro-cliché improperly ties
Lythrum to the enemy, the anthem in the killer
Mirror's ransom.) The seven 1s and seven 0s
Farm retaliation, run aground these *billet-
Doux* encrusted mines of tried and true.

Dear mid-November blues in early April,

Thank you for sending us your odor. We appreciate disgust and discussed the chance to read it. Unfortunately, the piece isn't wooded, nor the doorway wooed. We hope the years are yours and there be three, but elsewhere.

Please note that we are currently accepting submissions for our bottles of what love cannot forgive with solider guest judges. You can send limitless soldiers!

Thanks again for your mild-mannered battles.

Sincerely,

The ungentle unguent

An Apoplectic Paean to San Miguel de Allende

A city's love is broken purity. The purest love destroys itself, available to all. A conch of piety compels the candy to be sweeter. By necessity, archangels travel more like man than sunlight here, time much more like seeds. *Elotes* erase terror, truth's groomsman. Church bells pillage conflict, their hemp. *Domingo* and *Lunes* hold hands before the *Museo Histórico*, an oceanic triumph. Ben shopped for chiffon reassurance. The green flapping of white wings caught the clouds' attention as they drifted underneath a convent. Hours fell apart as sunlight fell together on the *Jardín Botánico*. Stray dogs hid their frominess like overrated trees. And love can't help but bay like hedonistic yesterday. It's all just kind of daydreams reconciled with green, inconsolable stars, a place to sing more seconds than you'll live. The blocks are a slideshow of cobblestone chords and pastel melodies. A scoffer envies all it has to offer, the epitome of chapters.

La primavera trepa
los árboles con las manos
sangrando. Mi amor
espera en la hora verde.

To Build an Icebox

"You're not dead until you're warm and dead."
An old medical adage, origin unknown

     For temporary freezing
Look away from the eternal dream of winter.

     For temporary ice
Seek the empty fullness of a wind-chill like Winston Churchill.

     For temporary cold
Go tell the sun he's pretty cool in movies.

     For a momentary ice rink
Tell the river's driver the goldfishes' golden rule. To sink, just be sincere.

     For ad interim goose bumps
In Spokane, ride the spoken reborn words on freeborn winds.

     For a salon-quality, short-lived subzero bite
Forsake the dens of ends.

     For the same reason fire hurts –
To get your just deserts – is why you're here. Face-palm!

     For a transitory arctic
House, deflower your fixed points of support with the stiffest and remotest hose. Man up!

    To experience a bitter etiquette
Make a playmate of the daylight.

    If winter was alive
I would not use it for what I use it for!

    But why can't we be limited-
Edition friends? Our brumal sense of humor hurts what can't be hurt and hurts!

    For a rimy limerick
What do I know?

    To catch an uncommon cold,
If I live long enough, I'll use your manners' hammers. Keep your head down!

    For a passing two-dog night
Bark in a voice sweet with fear or wrangle howls against the truth. Go balls deep!

    For a substitute Siberia
In Chillicothe, tell yourself the messenger is chilliness. It's easy.

    But if pursuit finds no success
All-in in fugitive benumbedness, the only sharper pain is your reward.

Notes from a Textbook of Botanical Oncology

One in two plants will get cancer. And it's always one from a married couple. Staying single is known to impart immunity.

Flowers with vernation tumors are brought *Get Well* cards by bees. The hummingbirds raise money to pay for the surgery.

The branch knotted with malignant masses bargains with God, denies its condition, profanes the sun and soil, but acceptance comes when one morning it wakes to a nest a neighboring tree had lain in its bifurcation.

In some tree cultures a nest is akin to a ring, in others a halo.

Cacti are particularly vulnerable to a cancer of the needle. The price they pay for a life of succulence, the controversy being a matter of choice. The afflicted Saguaro one-by-one lowers its arms.

Cows in India worship the cachectic leaves of grass, believing their wasting a form of purification. The hagiographers of these grazers call the death martyrdom and a miracle.

Cows in America will separate the grass from its tumor by ruminating, return the cancer-free blade to its plot of meadow.

The mosses of all nations suffer survivor's guilt because epochs ago a fern ate from the Tree of Knowledge, but the mosses were spared.

Fruits and nuts can develop neoplasms. Humans pick them and bury them with their own dead, believing they are medicinal in the underworld.

When an animal gets cancer, all the plants it makes its home with absorb the evil of the disease. They hide the evil from earth in their impenetrable roots. This is why root cancer is the most painful and most common.

On First Looking into a Sculpture of the Song, "The World is Watching," by Two Door Cinema Club

For Corri

There's nothing pink that doesn't bleed without
A little love beside it. Choral, but the moon, is pink
Without those little lights that sparkle,
Aliens that bloom and travel.

    There's nothing pink with frost that
    Doesn't spurn the harvesting of moss,
    Or else I've sworn, and you are nearer still.

There's nothing pink that, definite, is bluer
Still than less macabre. There's nothing that,
In place of space, can reinstall a choral grace –

    But there are aliens, empty, dry
    And tirelessly; flotsam, stinky
    Properly, but not arresting
    Up there, in the heavens: pink
    And hairy stones.

There's nothing pink that isn't oft-
Oppressive, gall of thunder, bell
Of California's peal
And carnal, irresponsible
As little girls that thrash beside

The sharks that tumble out of space
Like aliens in tidal lock with something
Accidental, and, without appearance, so
That all things lost are gray.

Selected Poetry Titles Published by SurVision Books

Seeds of Gravity: An Anthology of Contemporary Surrealist Poetry from Ireland
Edited by Anatoly Kudryavitsky
ISBN 978-1-912963-18-8

Invasion: An Anthology of Ukrainian Poetry about the War
Edited by Tony Kitt
ISBN 978-1-912963-32-4

Noelle Kocot. *Humanity*
(New Poetics: USA)
ISBN 978-1-9995903-0-7

Marc Vincenz. *Einstein Fledermaus*
(New Poetics: USA)
ISBN 978-1-912963-20-1

Helen Ivory. *Maps of the Abandoned City*
(New Poetics: England)
ISBN 978-1-912963-04-1

Tony Kitt. *The Magic Phlute*
(New Poetics: Ireland)
ISBN 978-1-912963-08-9

Clayre Benzadón. *Liminal Zenith*
(New Poetics: USA)
ISBN 978-1-912963-11-9

Thomas Townsley. *Tangent of Ardency*
(New Poetics: USA)
ISBN 978-1-912963-15-7

Anton Yakovlev. *Chronos Dines Alone*
(Winner of James Tate Poetry Prize 2018)
ISBN 978-1-912963-01-0

Mikko Harvey & Jake Bauer. *Idaho Falls*
(Winner of James Tate Poetry Prize 2018)
ISBN 978-1-912963-02-7

John Bradley. *Spontaneous Mummification*
(Winner of James Tate Poetry Prize 2019)
ISBN 978-1-912963-13-3

John Thomas Allen. *Rolling in the Third Eye*
(Winner of James Tate Poetry Prize 2019)
ISBN 978-1-912963-15-7

Gary Glauber. *The Covalence of Equanimity*
(Winner of James Tate Poetry Prize 2019)
ISBN 978-1-912963-12-6

Charles Kell. *Pierre Mask*
(Winner of James Tate Poetry Prize 2019)
ISBN 978-1-912963-19-5

Charles Borkhuis. *Spontaneous Combustion*
(Winner of James Tate Poetry Prize 2021)
ISBN 978-1-912963-30-0

George Kalamaras. *That Moment of Wept*
ISBN 978-1-9995903-7-6

George Kalamaras. *Through the Silk-Heavy Rains*
ISBN 978-1-912963-28-7

Order our books from http://survisionmagazine.com/bookshop.htm

www.ingramcontent.com/pod-product-compliance
Lightning Source LLC
Chambersburg PA
CBHW061314040426
42444CB00010B/2635